About this Learning Guide

Shmoop Will Make You a Better Lover*
*of Literature, History, Poetry, Life...

Our lively learning guides are written by experts and educators who want to show your brain a good time. Shmoop writers come primarily from Ph.D. programs at top universities, including Stanford, Harvard, and UC Berkeley.

Want more Shmoop? We cover literature, poetry, bestsellers, music, US history, civics, biographies (and the list keeps growing). Drop by our website to see the latest.

www.shmoop.com

Table of Contents

Introduction

In a Nutshell

English author H.G. (that's Herbert George) Wells is often called "the father of science fiction" (a title he shares with Jules Verne). As you'll soon see, there's a good reason for giving Wells this lofty title. Martian invasions of planet earth? That would be Wells's idea – you might have seen it played out on the big screen in *The War of the Worlds* (based on Wells's book of the same name). Time machines that travel back into the past or far into the future? Also Wells's idea, which he put to fabulous use in *The Time Machine*. And besides those two books, Wells wrote several other often-imitated classics of sci-fi, including *The Island of Dr. Moreau* and *The Invisible Man*, just to name a few. You might have heard of his numerous lesser-known novels and short stories as well.

In "The Red Room," an 1894 short story that ranks among his most popular, Wells took a break from sci-fi to foray into a genre already very popular in his day: the Gothic horror story. As he often did, Wells came up with a premise that influenced many later works of fiction, pulp fiction, and pop culture: a guy decides to spend the night in a haunted room to prove it's not haunted. All of the staples and stereotypes of the genre are here. We have an abandoned mansion with a tragic history, creepy people uttering dire warnings, a big, dark, and foreboding room lit by candlelight that casts lifelike shadows, and even some literal "bumps in the night." If you want a scary story to tell in the dark, with all the Gothic bells and whistles, "The Red Room" would be a good pick.

But this isn't your average piece of vintage Victorian horror. Though Wells uses the trappings of a ghost story, "The Red Room" is much less about ghosts than about human psychology. Wells himself had a pronounced skepticism about anything "supernatural." In many ways, he was like the narrator of this story. He's not the type of guy to take any Gothic ghost stories seriously, and to some extent, you might even read "The Red Room" as a demolition job on the genre (or perhaps a satire). Wells *does* take one thing very seriously in the story, though: the great power of fear to overwhelm human reason and self-control, no matter how resolute it might be. As the story's famous ending suggests, fear can haunt the human soul without the aid of any ghost.

Why Should I Care?

"The Red Room" is about something we've all experienced: fear. Particularly, that nasty kind you can't get rid of even when you know there's supposedly nothing to fear. Perhaps you were once terrified of a monster under your bed. Maybe you were afraid of the dark, or still are. (Heck, the narrator of this story certainly is afraid of the dark and he's 28.) Maybe you've actually been dared to spend a night in a "haunted" room or an abandoned farmhouse before and were horribly spooked. Or perhaps more ordinary: that upcoming violin recital you're dreading weeks in advance.

The point is we almost all have "irrational" fears, which still scare the pants off us. And that puts

us in the shoes of this story's narrator. He decides to spend the night in the haunted red room, because he knows there are no ghosts and wants to prove his point. In other words, he's in a situation where his good-sense and his clear-headed reason tell him there's nothing to fear. He believes he can confidently master any irrational fear he might feel. It turns out that he's in for a surprise.

Is there really anything to be afraid of there in the red room? You should read the story and answer that for yourself. But what author H.G. Wells really wants to get us thinking about is what it means to be afraid. He reminds us that fear itself can be extremely dangerous. It won't vanish in the face of reasoning or willpower, as we would like it to. Instead, it can make us lose control of ourselves, even hurt ourselves, and that's legitimately scary. Which is why, as the story would have it, fear is not all that unlike a ghost, always threatening to overwhelm human beings' rationality and crush their best-laid plans.

Anyway, that's the serious side. For those of you who like a classic horror story and have read your Edgar Allan Poe cover to cover, it's worth checking out "The Red Room." You've all the classic components of that genre right here, but with a twist. And it' just plain fun, like any good spine-tingler.

Summary

Book Summary

The story begins with the narrator, who's standing by a fire in an unknown room, confidently announcing to a couple of rather creepy elderly people that he's never seen a ghost and is not easily frightened. These creepy people – a man with a withered arm and an older woman – warn the narrator ominously that he's doing whatever it is he's doing (we don't know the details yet) by his own choosing.

The sense of foreboding increase when another even more ghoulish old man suddenly appears. This "man with the shade" (7) enters the room and coughs up a storm. In the midst of a tense silence, the narrator asks to be shown to the haunted room. The man with the withered arm tells him to take the candle outside the door. If the narrator wants to go to "the red room" on "this night of all nights" (16, 23), says the old man, he'll have to go alone.

That's fine with the narrator, who gets directions from the man with the withered arm, goes out the door, grabs the candle, and leaves the others behind. A walk up a spiral staircase, through a long, moonlit passageway, and up a small flight of stairs leads him to the door of the red room.

We learn from the narrator, who's already grown a little jumpy, that he is in Lorraine Castle. It's been abandoned for eighteen months, since "her ladyship" left it behind. (We learn that the old people are the custodians, or caretakers, of the castle.) Apparently there have been many little incidents in this haunted, red room, dating back to the "tragic end" (31) of a joke played by a husband on his young wife there long ago. Most recently, a young duke died while trying to spend a night in the haunted room. This news doesn't bode well for our narrator, who is trying

to do just what the duke did.

The narrator enters the red room, which is large, dark, and full of black and red furnishings and creepy shadows. He walks round of the room with his candle, the only source of light, to see it more closely. Along the way, he lights six candles he finds at various spots. He also lights the fireplace, which had been prepared by one of the custodians.

Once the room is illuminated, and he's set up a nice chair and table for himself near the fireplace, the narrator feels significantly better. But there are still some rather disturbing shadows at the other end of the room in a "dark alcove" that remind him of a "living, lurking thing" (33). So he places his candle in the alcove. Still rather jumpy, he decides it would be nice to have more light in the room, and remembers some other candles he'd seen in the hallway. He returns with ten more candles and puts them all over the room.

All is well until sometime past midnight, when the candle in the dark alcove is suddenly extinguished. As the narrator gets up to go relight it with his matches, two candles behind him also go dark. What's happening? A struggle then ensues as the narrator tries to keep the candles in the room lit as they mysteriously wink out, one by one. Although he appears to succeed for a while, particularly once he gives up on his matches and starts using a candle to light the others, it's a losing battle. Eventually, he trips and falls near the table, loses his candle, and finds himself in a room totally dark except for the dim glow of the fireplace. As he picks up a candle and approaches the fire to light it, even the fire is mysteriously extinguished.

By this time, the narrator has lost any sense of calm he had remaining, and makes a run for the door. However, it's dark and he can't see well, so he trips over the bed. He then gets "battered" (46) by various things in the dark, though it's unclear whether he's running into things, or something is actually battering him. He is eventually knocked unconscious cold by a blow on the forehead.

The narrator awakens to find that it is daytime, and that he doesn't remember what happened the night before. The custodians are taking care of him, and tell him about the red room. They'd found him at dawn, they say, with blood on his forehead. Recovering his memory, the narrator announces to them that he now knows the room is haunted. They are eager to know who haunts it – is it the old earl or his young wife? The narrator says the room is haunted by something far worse: Fear itself (with a capital "F"). Bringing the story to a grim close, the man with the shade proclaims that he knew as much, and that the room will remain haunted by black Fear "so long as this house of sin endures" (60).

"The Red Room"

- We jump right into the story as the narrator assures someone that "it will take a very tangible ghost to frighten" him (1). He stands up (in front of a fire) to prove his point.
- "The man with the withered arm," an older guy, is apparently one of the people our narrator is attempting to convince. The man tells the narrator that it's his own choice.
- The narrator responds that he's twenty years old and never seen a ghost. (So we learn that he's a skeptic.)

- There's also an old woman in the room, staring into the fire. She tells the narrator he's "never seen the likes of this house" either (4), and that there's still much in the world for him to see, especially given his young age. She sounds as if she's seen some freaky things in her day.
- The narrator assures them that he is approaching the evening with an "open mind" (5), and the man with the withered arm ominously warns him that it's his own choosing again.
- Another elderly man comes in, more ominous looking than the first guy. He has yellow teeth, a crutch, and a cough. He also has a shade over his eyes, and so will be known from now on as "the man with the shade."
- The man with the withered arm gives the man with the shade a nasty look as he sits down at a table.
- The narrator has another exchange with the man with the withered arm and which leads the man with the shade (who hadn't seen him) to notice his presence.
- The man with the shade is coughing all over the place. The narrator is rather disgusted by all of these.
- The narrator announces that he will happily make himself comfortable in "the haunted room" (12) if someone shows him to it. No one says anything, and the man with the shades just coughs some more.
- The narrator repeats himself.
- The man with the withered arm tells him there's a candle sitting outside the door. But, he says, if the narrator wants to go to "the red room" tonight, he's going to have to go alone.
- The old woman even throws in a "This night of all nights!" (16, 23) to make this scene even more terrifying and dramatic.
- The narrator has no problem with going alone, and asks for directions to the red room, which the man with the withered arm gives. The directions involve a spiral staircase and a long corridor, which, as we all know, are both extraordinarily creepy.
- The old woman again exclaims, "This night of all nights!" and the man with the shade asks the narrator if he's really going.
- Yes, the narrator is really going, even "this night of all nights." It's why he came here. He bids them good-bye and walks out the door, taking the candle.
- The narrator walks to the spiral staircase, and goes up the stairs. All the while he's thinking about how creepy and otherworldly the older people are. They freak him out, in spite of himself.
- As the narrator ascends the spiral staircase, we learn that we're in a castle, left behind by "her ladyship" (28).
- The narrator enters the long corridor, lit by the moonlight. Everything's just where it was left when it was deserted eighteen months before. Hmm…
- Seeing what looks like a person up ahead in the dark, the narrator grips the revolver in his pocket. But the person turns out to be a statue.
- Going up a short set of stairs at the end of the hallway, the narrator arrives at the door of the red room. He enters.
- We get some more back-story: the narrator is in the Lorraine Castle, and a young duke recently died in the red room. He opened the door and fell down the steps. Apparently, the duke was trying to do what the narrator is doing now. Gulp.
- That's not the only frightening story about the room. There are older and creepier tales too.
- We get some vague mention of a "timid wife" whose husband's joke intended to spook her

- came to a "tragic end" (31).
- That was how the red room supposedly got its reputation.
- The red room is big, dark, and creepy. It has "shadowy window bays" and "black corners" with "germinating darkness" (31).
- The narrator starts to walk around and check out the room with only his solitary candle to light the way.
- As the narrator makes his "systematic examination" (i.e., walks around and checks out the room), he lights the various candles he finds in front of the room's two big mirrors and on the mantelshelf. The fireplace has been prepared, so he lights that too.
- The narrator sets up a chair and a table before the fireplace and surveys the room with his back to the fire.
- It's better lit now, but the "shadow in the alcove at the end of the room" (33) still makes him nervous. He has the uneasy feeling that there's some "living, lurking thing" (33) in the alcove, so he walks over with his candle and leaves his candle there.
- The narrator admits his nerves are on edge, but also assures us that he is clear-headed and aware that nothing supernatural is going to happen. Nonetheless, he says little rhymes to himself to get over his nerves. It doesn't seem to work.
- Even with seven candles set up, the shifting shadows of the room are still making the narrator nervous, so he goes out into the hallway and rounds up ten more candles. He then sets them up so that every part of the room is illuminated by at least one candle. He is reassured.
- Sometime past midnight, the candle in the dark alcove of possibly "living, lurking things" goes out suddenly.
- Surprised, the narrator gets up from the table where he's been sitting and goes over to the candle to relight it with his matches.
- As he does, the two candles on the fireplace are extinguished.
- As the narrator goes to attend to them with his matches, the candles in front of one of the mirrors go out, "as if the wicks had been suddenly nipped between a finger and a thumb" (39).
- The candle at the foot of the bed follows suit, as does another candle on the mantelshelf.
- Getting a little hysterical and hand-shaky now (which interferes with his match lighting abilities), the narrator tries to relight the candles as others get extinguished.
- It looks like he's making gains when four more candles suddenly wink out on their own.
- The two candles on the table go out as the narrator stands aghast. He cries out in terror.
- Since those matches aren't working so well, the narrator drops them and takes up a candlestick, so he can relight the candles without worrying about striking a match each time.
- But the candles keep getting extinguished.
- Running from one candle to another frantically, the narrator tries to resist the "remorseless advance" (43) of darkness. He becomes disheveled, starts panting, and loses his self-possession in the process.
- The narrator bruises himself on the table, stumbles to the ground, and drops his candle. He picks up another, but it is blown out as well. The last two candles in the room are extinguished.
- There's still one last hope – the fire.
- The narrator approaches the fireplace and thrusts his candle in the grill...but the flames vanish.

- The room is completely dark, and the narrator has become irrational with fear.
- He makes a run for the door, but slams into the corner of the bed, and then gets more and more battered in the darkness, crying wildly all the while.
- A heavy blow on the narrator's forehead knocks him out cold.
- He falls, and then "remembers no more" (46).
- The narrator awakens to find that it is day, and that his head is bandaged.
- The man with the withered arm is watching him, and the old woman is pouring out some medicine for him. He tells them he can't remember who they are.
- The other two tell him of the red room. They'd found him at dawn, with blood on his forehead.
- The narrator begins to recover his memory, and the man with the withered arm asks him if he now believes that the room is haunted.
- Yes, the narrator does believe the room is haunted.
- The man with the withered arm admits that he wants to know who haunts it, since none of them have ever dared to see for themselves.
- The narrator says that neither the earl nor his countess – the suggestions of the man with the withered arm and the old woman – haunt the room. It isn't haunted by any ghost at all.
- It is something "worse, far worse" (55).
- What is it? Everyone wants to know.
- Fear, says the narrator. Dramatic silence ensues.
- The man with the shade then sighs and speaks up to say that he knew it. "There is Fear in that room of hers – black Fear, and there will be – so long as this house of sin endures" (60).
- And with that, the story ends.

Themes

Theme of Fear

Fear is the central theme of "The Red Room." The narrator of the story challenges himself to spend a night in a supposedly haunted room. Everyone else is terrified of the red room, but he confidently announces that he will prove that the room isn't haunted. He himself doesn't believe in anything supernatural, and is certain that his reason and good sense will conquer whatever irrational fears he might have. However, his fear turns out to be much stronger than he originally realizes: it can't be controlled by his intellect. As the story progresses, the narrator's fear gets stronger until it completely overwhelms his self-control. Fear is clearly the antagonist of the story. At the end, fear is revealed as a dangerous force, akin to an evil spirit, which counts among the greatest enemies of any human being.

Questions About Fear

1. What are the sources or causes of the narrator's fear? Is there one that seems primary?
2. How does the narrator try to control his fear? Which methods, if any, are successful, and which are not?

3. Is the narrator's fear in his head? Is it outside of him? What does it mean to say fear *haunts* the red room?
4. In what ways is fear like a ghost or a spirit? Why is it the "worst of all things that haunts mortal man"? (57)

Chew on Fear

The narrator's fear is both in his head and in the room itself, because it is the rooms' suggestiveness that creates his fear.

The main source of the narrator's fear is his overactive imagination.

Theme of The Supernatural

"The Red Room" is something of a ghost story – after all, it is about a young man's stay in a haunted room – so the supernatural is certainly an important theme. The young man, (a.k.a. the narrator), is an adamant skeptic of all things supernatural, and considers all superstition to be he product of a bygone age and "dead brains" (like those of the old custodians he meets). He wants to prove there's nothing supernatural about the red room. After the night is over, he still seems to stick to his story that there's no ghost. Enough odd things happen over the course of the night that it's possible to wonder if he saw a ghost after all. At moments, he certainly sounds as if he believes he's seeing one.

Questions About The Supernatural

1. So, we're dying to know, is there really a ghost in the story? Is there any evidence one-way or another? What can you find?
2. Do you think the narrator believes he encountered a ghost in the red room at the end? How about when he's actually in the room? Are there any moments when it appears he might have?
3. Do you think the narrator's understanding of the supernatural has changed by the end of the story? (Hint: Even if he still doesn't believe in ghosts, this doesn't necessarily mean his understanding hasn't changed.)

Chew on The Supernatural

The red room is really haunted by a ghost, as that's the only explanation for why the candles are extinguished.

The narrator never believes at any point in the story that there's a ghost in the room.

Theme of Versions of Reality

One of the primary sources of the fear that overwhelms the narrator of "The Red Room" is his active imagination. Alone in the red room, he certainly begins to see "suggestive" things around

him. The narrator claims he doesn't believe in ghosts or spirits; but his rational intellect is clearly no obstacle to his imagination. The old custodians he meets appear spectral and sinister, he hears and sees mysterious things in the dark, and the shadows around him seem to come alive. At some points, it even starts to look as if he no longer knows exactly what he's seeing. At the end, we're left wondering how much of what he actually perceived in the story was real, and how much was imagined. Or is it too hard to tell the difference?

Questions About Versions of Reality

1. Does the narrator's imagination seem overactive, or is it understandable in the circumstances in which he finds himself? Why?
2. How much of the creepiness of the castle is due to the narrator's imagination, and how much is "real"?
3. Is the narrator a reliable narrator? In other words, can his accounts of his experiences be trusted? Why or why not?

Chew on Versions of Reality

The narrator's imagination is overactive, and this makes him particularly susceptible to fear.

The narrator is not a reliable source of information.

Theme of Good vs. Evil

The narrative of "The Red Room" can be read as a classic good vs. evil story. More accurately, it could be seen as a battle of the forces of light against the powers of darkness. The nifty thing is that we're really talking about light vs. dark. The story centers on the struggle of the protagonist to preserve light in a room against the growing darkness, which threatens to extinguish it. The darkness and shadows are personified as an evil force, and they're closely tied to fear. (For more on fear as antagonist, check out "Character Roles.") The internal conflict of the narrator's reason against his fear mirrors the external conflict against the darkness of the red room.

Questions About Good vs. Evil

1. In what ways is literal darkness representative of evil, and literal light of good?
2. How could such abstract things be seen as "active" forces in the story?
3. What is the relationship between internal and external conflict in the story? Between fear and darkness?
4. Is the narrator himself a good character? Why or why not?

Chew on Good vs. Evil

The narrator is not a good character; he is the site for the real battle between good (reason) and evil (fear).

Quotes

Fear Quotes

"I can assure you," said I, "that it will take a very tangible ghost to frighten me." And I stood up before the fire with my glass in my hand. (1)

Thought: In the story's opening line, the narrator boasts that he's not easily frightened. That he says this as he is standing up, adds a bit of swagger. He's either a genuinely confident soul, or a poser. This opening line immediately sets up the plot as a contest of the narrator against his himself. This opening line is also ironic: as it turns out, it won't take anything "tangible" (that is, touchable) to frighten him at all.

A bronze group stood upon the landing, hidden from me by the corner of the wall, but its shadow fell with marvelous distinctness upon the white paneling, and gave me the impression of someone crouching to waylay me. I stood rigid for half a minute perhaps. Then, with my hand in the pocket that held my revolver, I advanced, only to discover a Ganymede and Eagle glistening in the moonlight. That incident for a time restored my nerve, and a porcelain Chinaman on a buhl table, whose head rocked silently as I passed him, scarcely startled me. (29)

Thought: We've already seen that the narrator is unnerved by the older people and the rustling he hears at the top of the stairs, but this is the first instance in which he's genuinely scared. How do we know? He has to "recover his nerve." It starts to look as if our narrator might be more easily spooked than he originally reveals. And what scares him in this case? It's the appearance of an everyday object as something threatening in the dark.

Here it was, thought I, that my predecessor was found, and the memory of that story gave me a sudden twinge of apprehension. (30)

Thought: The narrator admits to experiencing another pang of fear here, again before he enters the red room. This time what inspires his fear is not something he sees, but an *association* he has with the red room: it's where someone died, and there's a legend around it.

And there were other and older stories that clung to the room, back to the half-credible beginning of it all, the tale of a timid wife and the tragic end that came to her husband's jest of frightening her. (31)

Thought: More on the red room's dark history. Its reputation is a large part of what makes it a place steeped in fear. What's particularly interesting about this passage, however, is that we learn that the place first became cursed when the young countess came to a tragic end. And how did she come to a tragic end? She was frightened (though we don't know how) by her husband. The old woman makes significant mention of her being frightened again at the end of the story (48). So at the very beginning of the red room's black history, there's fear.

I resolved to make a systematic examination of the place at once, and dispel the fanciful suggestions of its obscurity before they obtained a hold upon me. (32)

Thought: The narrator is worried about the "the fanciful suggestions of [the red room's] obscurity." In other words, he's worried that the suggestive figures taken by the shadows ("fanciful suggestions") and general surrounding darkness ("obscurity") will spook him. In this sense, we see an admission that his fear is within his control (i.e., it's something that can "get a hold" of him). There's also the suggestion that fear isn't just something "in one's head"; the fear in him is brought about by something out there, by the darkness of the room itself. So what threatens him is both "inside" and "outside" him.

By this time I was in a state of considerable nervous tension, although to my reason there was no adequate cause for the condition. My mind, however, was perfectly clear. I postulated quite unreservedly that nothing supernatural could happen, and to pass the time I began to string some rhymes together, Ingoldsby fashion, of the original legend of the place. A few I spoke aloud, but the echoes were not pleasant. (34)

Thought: Here the narrator admits that he's starting to get nervous about the situation. Not only that, he also admits that there's a separation between the state of his nerves and that of his mind. His "reason" is perfectly clear; there is nothing to fear rationally. His reason doesn't have an effect on his nerves, however, which are beginning to give way. He needs to find other measures of comforting himself.

"Steady on!" I said. "These candles are wanted," speaking with a half-hysterical facetiousness, and scratching away at a match the while for the mantel candlesticks. My hands trembled so much that twice I missed the rough paper of the matchbox. (42)

Thought: The narrator is "half-hysterical." He's talking to himself, and starting to get funny ("facetious") in that odd way one does as one begins to lose it. He's also having trouble controlling his body: his hands are trembling. Since he needs his hands to cooperate if he's going to relight those candles, he's not in a good situation.

I was now almost frantic with the horror of the coming darkness, and my self-possession deserted me. (43)

Thought: Here we have it: the narrator's lost control of himself because of his terror. Not only is that cool, rational approach gone, but he can't even control his body. He's entering a frenzy, in which he'll act without thinking. This raises an interesting question: when we say the narrator's "losing control of himself," what exactly do we mean? Can we no longer hold him responsible for what he's doing? Is he doing it?

...as I thrust the candle between the bars darkness closed upon me like the shutting of an eye, wrapped about me in a stifling embrace, sealed my vision, and crushed the last vestiges of reason from my brain. The candle fell from my hand. I flung out my arms in a vain effort to thrust that ponderous blackness away from me, and, lifting up my voice, screamed with all my might--once, twice, thrice. (45)

Thought: "Reason" has left the building at this point. The narrator has completely lost it. This is the moment when his terror is at its worst. He does what people often do in complete terror: he screams. We've come a long way from what he said at the beginning of the story, haven't we.

"The worst of all the things that haunt poor mortal man," said I; "and that is, in all its nakedness--Fear that will not have light nor sound, that will not bear with reason, that deafens and darkens and overwhelms. It followed me through the corridor, it fought against me in the room----" (57)

Thought: Here we have the narrator's dramatic announcement that *Fear* is what haunts the red room. Whereas before he was dismissive of fear, he is now terrified of it. He's had a firsthand experience of its power. Fear has the power to make a person lose control of himself. It doesn't respond to reason. It's a real *invisible* enemy, just like a ghost would be (that's part of what makes it so scary). The narrator even goes so far as to identify fear as an enemy of mankind.

The Supernatural Quotes

"Eight-and-twenty years," said I, "I have lived, and never a ghost have I seen as yet." (3)

Thought: The narrator makes clear early on that he's skeptical of ghosts. This immediately makes the reader wonder whether his opinion will change before the night is over, setting off the story's supernatural thread. The narrator's mention of his age also makes it easy to peg him as an inexperienced whippersnapper who doesn't believe in ghosts. Which is what the old woman does. So this comment also triggers the old vs. young contrast of the story.

Well," I said, "if I see anything to-night, I shall be so much the wiser. For I come to the business with an open mind." (5)

Thought: The narrator claims that he's "open-minded" on the subject of ghosts. But this isn't true, as we see from his reaction to the older people. Maybe he's just saying it to appease his audience.

They seemed to belong to another age, an older age, an age when things spiritual were different from this of ours, less certain; an age when omens and witches were credible, and ghosts beyond denying. Their very existence was spectral; the cut of their clothing, fashions born in dead brains. (28)

Thought: Here is where we see the judgmental side of the narrator. He thinks that any belief in the "supernatural" is an obsolete superstition from a past age. The old people belong to that age. He doesn't. In his opinion, they have "dead brains." In other words, no rational or sensible person would believe in ghosts or goblins.

That had been the end of his vigil, of his gallant attempt to conquer the ghostly tradition of the place, and never, I thought, had apoplexy better served the ends of superstition. (31)

Thought: It's clear that the young duke who died had been involved in a project similar to the narrator's: proving the red room isn't haunted, by making it through the night. The narrator admires the duke's project (he thinks it was a "valiant" attempt). This gives us insight into the narrator's own motivation. It's also worth noting that the narrator explains the young duke's death in a way that excludes any role of the supernatural. The narrator claims the duke had "apoplexy" and fell down the stairs. We get the sense he resents the fact that the duke's death has been ascribed to the ghost, and used to support the very superstition against which the duke fought. What's apoplexy, by the way? Well, it can be a lot of things: a stroke, a hemorrhage, or just a fit of some kind. Maybe, in this case, it's a fit caused by fear.

My mind, however, was perfectly clear. I postulated quite unreservedly that nothing supernatural could happen, and to pass the time I began to string some rhymes together, Ingoldsby fashion, of the original legend of the place. A few I spoke aloud, but the echoes were not pleasant. For the same reason I also abandoned, after a time, a conversation with myself upon the impossibility of ghosts and haunting. (34)

Thought: Even as he' starting to suffer "considerable nervous tension," the narrator is still sticking confidently to his rejection of anything supernatural. That's his reason talking, and it's just as sure of itself as ever. It doesn't seem to be having much of an effect on his fear, though.

The one in the alcove flared in a draught, and the fire-flickering kept the shadows and penumbra perpetually shifting and stirring. (35)

Thought: This is important bit of information: it tells us there's a draft (the British spelling is "draught") in the room. Moreover, this draft seems to be most pronounced in the alcove. Could that be what causes the alcove candle, and possibly the others, to go out? At this point, the narrator's quite happy to explain the candles' behavior with the draught.

The flame vanished, as if the wicks had been suddenly nipped between a finger and a thumb, leaving the wick neither glowing nor smoking, but black. (39)

Thought: The narrator states outright that it *looks* as if someone put the candle out, because the way the it goes out doesn't look like wind. Are his eyes testifying to something supernatural at this point? On the one hand, he only says it's "as if" the wicks had been nipped out by a hand. On the other, he uses stronger language beforehand ("there was no mistake about it"). What does he actually think has caused the candle to go out at this point? What do you think about it?

But then in a volley there vanished four lights at once in different corners of the room, and I struck another match in quivering haste, and stood hesitating whither to take it. (42)

Thought: By this time, the situation *definitely* looks fishy. How would four candles in different corners of the room go out at once? That would be a pretty odd thing for wind to do, since it usually comes from one direction. And it wouldn't make sense to say the narrator's motion put them out either, since they're so far apart. Is there really a ghost here?

As I stood undecided, an invisible hand seemed to sweep out the two candles on the table. (43)

Thought: Again the narrator uses the language of some "invisible hand" seeming to put out the candles. He thinks that what he's seeing, (i.e., the candles going out), is best explained with reference to something invisible. It almost seems as if the most rational thing to believe in this circumstance is that there is a ghost. Or rather, it would be, if you believed ghosts existed.

"Yes," said I; "the room is haunted." (51)

Thought: When the narrator says this, it sounds as if he's recanted on his skepticism, and now believes in ghosts after all. Of course, shortly afterwards he changes the meaning of what he says by specifying that the room is haunted by fear, and not by a ghost. That seems to answer the question of whether there's anything supernatural in the story (especially since the man with the shades agrees with him). But how does the narrator really know that? He still hasn't explained how the rather improbable thing with the candles happened.

Versions of Reality Quotes

A monstrous shadow of him crouched upon the wall and mocked his action as he poured and drank. (11)

Thought: This is the very first instance of a "suggestive shadow" in the story. Not only is the shadow "monstrous," but the description of it as "mocking" the man with the shade (it's his shadow) almost makes it seem independent of him. Even this early in the story, the narrator's imagination is already starting to take on a life of its own. (Of course, a description like this also adds to the general ambience of creepiness for the reader.)

I must confess that the oddness of these three old pensioners in whose charge her ladyship had left the castle, and the deep-toned, old-fashioned furniture of the housekeeper's room in which they foregathered, affected me in spite of my efforts to keep myself at a matter-of-fact phase... Their very existence was spectral; the cut of their clothing, fashions born in dead brains. (28)

Thought: A contrast between the narrator's "matter-of-fact" phase and his more "fanciful" imaginings about the "spectral" old people. The narrator thinks reality is straightforward, clear-cut, and not mysterious or suggestive. In his book, anything mysterious or suggestive must be a product of the human imagination, as all "supernatural" things are. But the narrator's imagination turns the old custodians into something suggestive – they become almost ghostly ("spectral") themselves.

I came to the landing and stopped there for a moment, listening to a rustling that I fancied I heard; then, satisfied of the absolute silence, I pushed open the baize-covered door and stood in the corridor. (28)

Thought: This is next instance of the narrator perceiving something suggestive, which may not be there. This could be read as more evidence that his imagination is acting up at this point. It's also worth noting that in this case the narrator thinks he hears something; most of the other perceptions are visual and not auditory.

A bronze group stood upon the landing, hidden from me by the corner of the wall, but its shadow fell with marvelous distinctness upon the white paneling, and gave me the impression of someone crouching to waylay me. I stood rigid for half a minute perhaps. (29)

Thought: It sounds like the narrator momentarily thinks that there really is someone crouching in the hallway. This is the most obvious case of the narrator "thinking he sees something" in the story. It also indicates how active his imagination is, and how fragile his nerves might be.

I resolved to make a systematic examination of the place at once, and dispel the fanciful suggestions of its obscurity before they obtained a hold upon me. (32)

Thought: The narrator wants to make sure that the "suggestions" made by the dark ("obscurity") don't get his imagination working actively. It is the dark specifically that he blames for stimulating his imagination. He blames the darkness this because it literally conceals things from sight (as it did with the Ganymede statue), and because it's ominous and murky. That's why he resolves to remove the element of mystery and murkiness in the room by removing the dark, first by making a survey of it with his candle.

My precise examination had done me good, but I still found the remoter darkness of the place, and its perfect stillness, too stimulating for the imagination. (33)

Thought: Another affirmation of the narrator. Apparently knowing what's "really" in the room isn't enough to prevent the narrator's imagination from conjuring up all kinds of things. There's still too much darkness in the room. He's got to work on that.

The shadow in the alcove at the end in particular, had that undefinable quality of a presence, that odd suggestion of a lurking, living thing, that comes so easily in silence and solitude. At last, to reassure myself, I walked with a candle into it, and satisfied myself that there was nothing tangible there. I stood that candle upon the floor of the alcove, and left it in that position. (33)

Thought: The great description of the "lurking, living" shadow. Here the narrator's imagination is making scary things out of the darkness again. He tries to put it to rest by going to the alcove and confirming there's nothing there. But that's not quite enough. To really quiet his imagination, the narrator needs to eliminate what it finds suggestive, namely, the dark.

The flame vanished, as if the wicks had been suddenly nipped between a finger and a thumb, leaving the wick neither glowing nor smoking, but black. (39)

Thought: Is the narrator's imagination being overly active again, and making figures out of the darkness? Or is there really something there? From what he tells us, we have no way of knowing.

I staggered back, turned, and was either struck or struck myself against some other bulky furniture. I have a vague memory of battering myself thus, to and fro in the darkness, of a cramped struggle, and of my own wild crying as I darted to and fro, of a heavy blow at last upon my forehead, a horrible sensation of falling that lasted an age, of my last frantic effort to keep my footing, and then I remember no more. (46)

Thought: At this point, we get a strong sense that the narrator's perceptions are no longer reliable. Not only is his memory foggy, (this is the only moment in the story when it becomes clear he's narrating *post facto* or after the fact), he also can't seem to decide whether he's running into things or whether something else strikes him.

I rolled my eyes into the corner, and saw the old woman, no longer abstracted, pouring out some drops of medicine from a little blue phial into a glass. (47)

Thought: The narrator sees the old woman "no longer abstracted." Now that it's day and the dreadful experience is behind him, he can recognize that she's not quite so creepy or abnormal as she appeared the night before. It might also help that she's taking care of him. In any case, this remark makes us wonder how much of what he described was "accurate," and how much

was produced by his state of mind.

Good vs. Evil Quotes

[…] I stood with the candle held aloft, surveying the scene of my vigil, the great red room of Lorraine Castle, in which the young duke had died. Or, rather, in which he had begun his dying, for he had opened the door and fallen headlong down the steps I had just ascended. That had been the end of his vigil, of his gallant attempt to conquer the ghostly tradition of the place. (31)

Thought: This passage makes the young duke out as something of a hero: he's "gallant." He was trying to fight against darkness, superstition, and the "ghostly tradition" of the castle. In other words, he was trying to be the good guy and do battle with the forces of darkness. But he died. Whatever it is that's in the red room remains.

My candle was a little tongue of light in its vastness, that failed to pierce the opposite end of the room, and left an ocean of mystery and suggestion beyond its island of light. (31)

Thought: This is the most suggestive piece of light/darkness imagery in the story. It conveys the sense that the darkness is something overwhelming, and the light just a small blip in the midst of it. It's literal in this case, but there's definitely something symbolic about it too. The narrator, with his candle, is the bearer of light in the midst of an enormous darkness. Feels rather threatening.

The shadow in the alcove at the end in particular, had that undefinable quality of a presence, that odd suggestion of a lurking, living thing, that comes so easily in silence and solitude. At last, to reassure myself, I walked with a candle into it, and satisfied myself that there was nothing tangible there. I stood that candle upon the floor of the alcove, and left it in that position. (33)

Thought: The darkness in the red room threatens the narrator and feels alive. It "lurks." He tries to fight it off by combating it with light, in the form of the candle. At this point, the literal struggle between light and dark in the red room begins (and with it, the more suggestive struggle between the narrator and some "dark power").

These I put in various knick-knacks of china with which the room was sparsely adorned, lit and placed where the shadows had lain deepest, some on the floor, some in the window recesses, until at last my seventeen candles were so arranged that not an inch of the room but had the direct light of at least one of them. It occurred to me that when the ghost came, I could warn him not to trip over them. The room was know quite brightly illuminated. There was something very cheery and reassuring in these little streaming flames, and snuffing them gave me an occupation, and afforded a helpful sense of the passage of time. (35)

Thought: For a while, all is well. The narrator appears to have satisfactorily conquered the darkness of the red room – and his own fear – by filling the place with candles. The light is "cheery and reassuring."

Then something happened in the alcove. I did not see the candle go out, I simply turned and saw that the darkness was there, as one might start and see the unexpected presence of a stranger. The black shadow had sprung back to its place. (37)

Thought: When the "black shadow" springs into place, it's as if the force of darkness that was originally in the red room has reasserted itself. It suggestively reappears in exactly the spot that had most disturbed the narrator originally: the alcove opposite the fireplace. You might call that spot the "locus of darkness." That's where the darkness "comes from," and where it seems strongest.

While I stood gaping, the candle at the foot of the bed went out, and the shadows seemed to take another step towards me. (39)

Thought: The darkness, in the form of the shadows, advances. The language here really makes it sound as if a battle is ensuing between the narrator and some living, evil force that's coming toward him.

[…] but for all that the steady process of extinction went on, and the shadows I feared and fought against returned, and crept in upon me, first a step gained on this side of me and then on that. I was now almost frantic with the horror of the coming darkness, and my self-possession deserted me. (43)

Thought: This time the image of a "battle" between the narrator with his light and the advancing shadows is made explicit with the word "fought." The shadows are the narrator's enemy. He fears them, and they are gaining on him. The image of a storm cloud sweeping out the stars is particularly powerful.

I leaped panting from candle to candle, in a vain struggle against that remorseless advance. (43)

Thought: Here again we see language suggestive of a battle, a "remorseless advance" of the enemy. Now it definitely looks as if the narrator is losing.

I flung out my arms in a vain effort to thrust that ponderous blackness away from me, and, lifting up my voice, screamed with all my might – once, twice, thrice. (45)

Thought: The narrator has lost. The darkness has eliminated all light, overwhelmed him, and now surrounds him completely. His wits are gone. The image of the screaming narrator flinging his arms around conveys complete helplessness.

"I knew that was it. A power of darkness. To put such a curse upon a home! It lurks there always. (60)

Thought: The man with the shades, unlike the narrator, calls fear a "power of darkness." Although fear was already personified in the narrator's description, the old man's use of the supernatural-sounding (and very Gothic) phrase makes it even clearer that fear is an active evil. It also brings out the tight connection between the fear the narrator was feeling and the literal "darkness" against which he fought in the red room. This is a great wrap up for the story.

Plot Analysis

Classic Plot Analysis

Initial Situation
He's sure going to show that ghost…
The narrator begins the story by boldly announcing his disbelief in ghosts and his intention to stay in the haunted red room. His determination to prove that the red room isn't haunted sets up the story. The old custodians help create a sense of foreboding by repeatedly saying things like, "This night of all nights!" (16, 23) and "It's of your own choosing!" (2, 6, 8, 26). The stage concludes when the narrator gets instructions to the red room, and sets off on his adventure.

Conflict
This castle is creepier than he thought
No sooner is the narrator out of the housekeepers' room than he begins to feel spooked in spite of himself. There's the noise he thinks he hears on the staircase, and the episode with the Ganymede statue, which causes him to finger his revolver. He goes to the red room, and finds it dark. The narrator is unnerved by all the shadows, particularly in that nasty little alcove at one end of the room. He deals with the alcove by putting a candle in it, and then runs with the idea, filling the room with candles and seemingly settling into it. So far, so good.

Complication
Candles do the darnedest things
The narrator's outpost against the darkness is jeopardized when the candle in the alcove goes out after midnight. When the narrator goes to put it out, two more go out. Here begins a sharp upswing in the tension of the story. A real struggle ensues as the narrator tries to keep the candles lit in the face of some force that's putting them out faster and faster. All the while, he's growing more unhinged; things do not look good for his self-control. He stumbles and falls.

Climax

The fire's gone, and so are his senses

Once all the candles are out, the narrator's last hope of keeping light in the room and calming his frayed nerves rests with the fire, which he approaches in desperation. But that "incontinent fire" is soon gone. And then "the last vestiges of reason" are "crushed" from his brain (45). The darkness has won, and the narrator fittingly screams wildly three time. There is nothing left to do but escape.

Suspense

Desperate dash to the door in the dark

The narrator makes a run for the door, but stumbles all over the place. He gets "battered" (46). It's not certain whether he's just running into things or if something is actually battering him. Will he make it? Nope. He bumps his head, and goes out like a…light.

Denouement

Morning After Realizations

There's a break in the story, because the narrator is unconscious. Everything resumes the next day. No more tension. The narrator is safe, out of the room, and being cared for by the old people (who look much better in the daylight). His memory's gone, but it slowly recovers, and all is explained. The older people reveal the state he was in when they found him. The narrator reveals what it is that haunts the room: Fear!

Conclusion

"There is Fear in that room of hers – black Fear, and there will be – so long as this house of sin endures" (60).

The man with the shade gets the last word. He repeats what the narrator says, only more eloquently and with greater finality. What's more, he undoubtedly does this in a deep and terrifying voice.

Booker's Seven Basic Plots Analysis: Overcoming the Monster

Anticipation Stage and "Call"

The narrator confidently announces he intends to stay in the red room to the old custodians; he is unfazed by their warnings.

By the beginning of the story, the narrator has already been "called." He's made up his mind to spend the night in the red room, to prove it's not haunted. The "monster" has also been identified as whatever haunts the red room. In this initial stage, we learn a bit more about his intentions and receive the warnings from the older people that he might get more than he bargained for in the red room. The narrator also receives instructions to the fateful spot from the man with the withered arm.

Dream Stage

The narrator makes his way to the red room, explores it, and makes himself at home as best he can.

Although the narrator becomes uneasy almost immediately after leaving the custodians' room,

things appear to go well at first. He gets to the red room without much trouble; he is able to control those small flare-ups of fear he has (with the Ganymede statue, for instance). Once in the room, he's unnerved by its creepiness and suggestive shadows, but is able to comfort himself by lighting the candles. There is no real sign of a monster at all.

Frustration Stage
The first candle goes out in the dark alcove; more follow in its footsteps.
From the start, the alcove has been the most sinister part of the red room. After all, it is the farthest from the light of the fire. So it makes sense that the first bit of funny business should happen in the alcove: a candle goes out, which is the first sign there might be a ghost. Then things become strange as "the monster" shows its face. From this point on, the narrator's comfort is gone, and he's locked in conflict with whatever it is that's putting out the candles. All the while he's losing control of himself. The real monster – Fear – has arrived in full force, coinciding with whatever it was that put out the candle (a draft? maybe really a ghost?).

Nightmare Stage
The fire goes out and the room goes black.
When the fire goes out and there is no light left in the room, the monster is at the height of its power. The darkness drives the narrator out of his mind with fear: he screams three times and makes a run for the door, crashing into all kinds of things. It's not clear if he'll escape. Then it all goes black. Admittedly, it's a brief nightmare stage.

The Thrilling Escape from Death and Death of the Monster
The narrator wakes up and reveals the identity of what haunts the red room.
We don't see a "thrilling escape" because the narrator's brief escape attempt ends as he loses consciousness. Fear "got" him. But our narrator does escape in a sense: he makes it through in one piece and is able to wake up the next morning outside of the red room. (That's better than we can say about the duke, who didn't make it out alive.) The narrator's "escape" mostly is due to the fact that the older people seem to be responsible for his survival. The monster doesn't "die" either, as the last remarks from the man with the shade reveal. The monster, a.k.a. fear, will be there until the house falls. Nonetheless, the narrator reveals the identity of the monster, and escapes with his life, even if he technically loses to the monster.

Three Act Plot Analysis

Act I
We meet the narrator, who proclaims confidently that ghosts don't scare him, because he doesn't believe in them. We meet the foreboding older custodians of the castle, who add to the general sense of dread. The narrator sets off for the red room, and gives us the back-story, (which isn't much). He arrives at the door of the red room and enters. There is no turning back now.

Act II
The narrator explores the red room and tries to make himself comfortable. To get rid of that spooky darkness, he sets up a few candles. Then he decides to battle darkness with light by

getting more candles. Man, this red room isn't so bad after all. Then the first candle goes out. The narrator's epic struggle with the dark begins…and ends in total blackness when the fire itself is extinguished.

Act III

His wits gone, the narrator rushes to the door, and gets beat up, although we're not sure how. He loses consciousness. Waking up the next morning, the narrator recovers his temporarily lost memory and all is explained. We learn that it is no ghost, but "fear" itself that haunts the room.

Study Questions

1. How would you explain what happens to the narrator in the red room? Do you think a ghost is responsible? If so, why? If not, what is it?
2. Do you think it makes sense to say the red room is haunted? (This may depend on your answer to the first question.) Do you buy the idea that it can still be haunted even if there's no ghost?
3. Is the narrator's descent into panic believable?
4. Can you imagine the narrator as a woman? How might she be different than our male narrator?
5. Is "The Red Room" best described as a horror story? Why or why not?
6. Do you think "The Red Room" is ever comical? What parts are humorous? Do you think it's intentional? Could the whole story even be funny?
7. Does "The Red Room" create suspense? If so, how? Is it actually scary? What do you think?

Characters

All Characters

The Narrator Character Analysis

The Narrator: Champion of Reason or Brash Young Whippersnapper?

From the very first line of the story, we get the sense that the narrator's a bit on the arrogant side.

"I can assure you," said I, "that it will take a very tangible ghost to frighten me." And I stood up

before the fire with my glass in my hand. (1)

Come on, he's just asking for it, isn't it?

Throughout his conversation with the old custodians at the start of the story, the narrator seems eager to make a point that he's not going to be scared by the red room. And what gives him his confidence? The fact that he knows better than to believe in ghosts. He's lived all of 28 years and "never has he seen a ghost yet" (3).

Sure, he claims to approach the situation with an "open mind" (5), but we know better. Once he's on his own he gives his real feelings about the custodians and their superstitious beliefs:

They seemed to belong to another age, an older age, an age when things spiritual were different from this of ours, less certain; an age when omens and witches were credible, and ghosts beyond denying. Their very existence was spectral; the cut of their clothing, fashions born in dead brains. (28)

The narrator's young age suits his self-image as modern fellow with up-to-date beliefs and a healthy sense of rational skepticism. By contrast, he believes that the old custodians believe in ghosts and magic because they have "dead brains" (28). And for the narrator, there's something worthy and admirable in trying to fight superstition. Although he never explicitly announces that he's come to the castle to prove it is not haunted (he just says he's there to stay the night in the red room), that's what we gather from his comment about the ill-fated young duke who tried the same thing:

That had been the end of his vigil, of his gallant attempt to conquer the ghostly tradition of the place, and never, I thought, had apoplexy better served the ends of superstition. (31)

The narrator admires the duke's attempt to dispel the myth of the haunted red room. He also ascribes his death to "apoplexy," which could mean any number of things, from a panic attack, to a stroke, or brain hemorrhage. What's for certain, though, is that the narrator doesn't think anything supernatural killed the duke, and finds it unfortunate that the duke's death should be used to continue the superstition. That's why he, the narrator, will try to dispel the idea that the red room is haunted on his own. Is he up to it?

As we'll see, in his character, the narrator plays out a more fundamental conflict between the force of reason and the power of fear. This conflict is really the central theme of the whole story.

The Narrator's Reason: Confident and Controlled

The narrator values "reason" both as a means of keeping oneself under control and as a way of looking at the world (i.e., taking account of facts only as they are). As he says leaving the custodians' room, he wants to keep himself "at a matter-of-fact phase" (28) – no vague imaginings or "irrational" superstitions (even though he lets his own mind contrive some pretty fanciful things about the custodians after saying this). He's very precise in his descriptions, and approaches his surroundings with an analytical frame of mind. Take the moment when he enters the red room, for instance:

I resolved to make a systematic examination of the place at once, and dispel the fanciful suggestions of its obscurity before they obtained a hold upon me. (33)

"Systematic examination"? (Later in the paragraph, he again emphasizes that it is a "precise" examination). The narrator seems to be just like a scientist, doesn't he? He approaches an environment by determining what is actually there as precisely as he can. Why? Because he figures that if he knows what's there, he'll know whether or not there's anything to fear. If there's not, he can dismiss any fear he feels, or any superstitious belief he might hold. (Note that he assumes that he'll be able to see whatever is "there.")

The narrator's rational approach to is connected to the imagery of lightness and darkness. (See "Symbols, Imagery, Allegory" for more on this theme.) Light reveals, and makes one aware of what's there in the first place. In so doing, light can eliminate fear by revealing that there is nothing to fear. On the other hand, darkness conceals or "obscures" objects. In the dark, one can't tell if anything is actually there. That's why the narrator uses light, literally, as a weapon against his fear. He wants to reveal whatever objects are in the room in order to prove to himself that there's nothing he need fear.

The Narrator's Nerves: Not the Strongest

In spite of his confidence and his resolution to be rational, the narrator gives us various indications that he doesn't have his own nerves under the best of control. Even before he's in the red room, he's starting to think he hears or sees things.

First, there's the "rustling" (28) he hears overhead when climbing the spiral stairs, which disappears when he stops to listen. Then, in the hallway, he's jumpy enough to take the Ganymede statue in the dark for somebody crouching, lying in wait for him. And then there are the shadows in the red room. Once he enters it and makes his rounds, he admits, "By this time I was in a state of considerable nervous tension, although to my reason there was no adequate cause for the condition" (34). The narrator is starting to become aware that his fear doesn't always respond to his reason or his will. Fear can operate on its own, and grab hold of him despite his best intentions.

As the night wears on, things begin to unravel. The light of the candles has kept his nerves under control. Once the first candle goes out after midnight, all other candles begin to do the same. All of his assurances that there's nothing to be afraid of and his systematic examination of the room prove useless. When the fire goes out, his fear conquers him completely, and his reason deserts him:

…as I thrust the candle between the bars darkness closed upon me like the shutting of an eye, wrapped about me in a stifling embrace, sealed my vision, and crushed the last vestiges of reason from my brain. (45)

His confidence, it would seem, is misplaced.

After a Night in the Red Room…

The narrator at the end of the story is a humbled version of the narrator we meet at the beginning. Regardless of the reason behind one's convictions, and regardless of whether

there's really anything to be afraid of in a given situation, he recognizes that fear is a concrete force to be reckoned with. It's not clear that a person can do anything about it, try though they might. Perhaps now he's more sympathetic to the old people. He does admit, when he awakens to the old woman, that she looks "no longer abstracted" (47). He's also willing to admit the room is haunted. Though at the end of the day, he still doesn't believe in ghosts.

The Narrator Timeline and Summary

- The narrator announces to the old custodians that he's not going to be easily scared by any ghost, and that he doesn't believe in ghosts in the first place.
- He affirms that he will spend the night in the red room.
- In spite of the warnings of the old custodians, the narrator holds firm in his intention to stay in the red room, and asks for directions to it.
- The narrator leaves the custodians behind in the housekeeper's room, takes a candle, and walks up the spiral staircase to the long passageway. He thinks about how strange the custodians are, and dismisses their superstitions.
- At the top of the stairs, he thinks he hears something, but listens and finds only silence.
- In the long passageway, the narrator encounters the Ganymede statue, and stands still. He is afraid it is someone lying in wait for him. He grasps his revolver. Then he recognizes what it is, and continues to the room.
- The narrator enters the red room and makes his "systematic examination" with his candle (32). No ghosts to be seen. He lights the candles in the room as he walks.
- The narrator lights the fire and sets himself up in front of it with a table and chair.
- Troubled by the shadows in the alcove at the other end of the room, the narrator walks over and sets his candle there.
- The shadows are gone.
- Inspired by that idea, the narrator goes back into the hallway to round up all the candles there. He sets them up throughout the room, which is now lit by seventeen candles total.
- After midnight, the candle in the alcove goes out, surprising the narrator. When he goes to light it, two other candles behind him go out.
- Going to light those two, the narrator sees more candles go out. He starts running around the room to keep the candles lit, and they start going out more quickly.
- Frustrated with his matches, the narrator grabs the bedroom candlestick to help him light the candles more quickly.
- The narrator stumbles and falls when he runs into the table, losing his candlestick. All of the lights are out except for the fire now. Then that goes out as he tries to light a candle in it.
- The narrator screams three times.
- The narrator makes a run for the door, crashing about and battering himself as he goes (and screaming more). He gets knocked out after a blow on the head.
- The next morning, the narrator awakens to find the custodians caring for him. He doesn't remember what happened.
- After being told about the red room and the condition in which he was found, the narrator's memory slowly comes back.

- He announces the red room is indeed haunted: by Fear.

The Man with the Shade Character Analysis

The man with the shade is the oldest and probably the creepiest of the three creepy old custodians. He comes into the custodians' quarters later (after the beginning of the story), which gives the narrator plenty of time to study him. We get the narrator's observations:

He supported himself by a single crutch, his eyes were covered by a shade, and his lower lip, half averted, hung pale and pink from his decaying yellow teeth. (7)

In the beginning of the story, the man with the withered arm doesn't say much, although he does cough and splutter a lot. At the very end, he's the one who speaks up and finishes the story with his pronouncement about "fear" and "this house of sin" (60). Unlike the other two custodians, he appears to have suspected it was fear that haunted the room, and not a ghost. Unlike the narrator at the beginning, however, he appears to have understood just how serious a force Fear is. Maybe he's the wisest of all.

The Man with the Shade Timeline and Summary

- The man with the shade comes into the custodians' room where the narrator and the other two custodians are gathered. He coughs up a storm and sits down clumsily, receiving a nasty look from the man with the withered arm.
- At the offer of the man with the withered arm, the man with the shade has a drink.
- The next morning, the man with the shade is with the narrator and the other two custodians, although we don't know of his presence until he speaks.
- After the narrator says the red room is haunted by fear, the man with the shade announces that he knew this all along. He claims that fear will not leave the room until the house itself is gone.

The Man with the Withered Arm Character Analysis

The man with the withered arm is another one of three old and creepy-looking custodians left to take care of the abandoned Lorraine Castle. He tries, and fails, to dissuade the narrator from going to the red room. The morning after the narrator's nasty night, the man with the withered arm cares for him with the old woman, and appears to have warmed to him somewhat after his bad experience. We don't know much about the man with the withered arm, except that he's afraid of the room and refuses to show the narrator there at night (although he does give him directions).

The Man with the Withered Arm Timeline and Summary

- At the story's beginning, the man with the withered arm tells the narrator that if he goes to the red room, "it's his choosing" (2, 6, 8, 26).
- When the narrator appears set on going to the red room, the man with the withered arm refuses to take him there.
- Instead, he gives the narrator directions.
- The next morning, the man with the withered arm is taking care of the narrator with the other two custodians. He wants to know if the narrator believes the room is haunted now, and the narrator tells him that he does.
- The man with the withered arm wants to know whether it's the old earl who haunts the room. No, says the narrator, it's fear.

The Old Woman Character Analysis

The old woman is the third in the trio of creepy old custodians. She has pale eyes and stares intently into the fire. Her most distinctive feature at the beginning is that she says "this night of all nights!" twice. She also warns the young narrator that he might not have lived long enough to see everything yet, ominously implying that there is more to see in life. Like the man with the withered arm, she's scared of the red room. Whereas the man with the withered arm thinks it's the earl who haunts the red room, the old woman is convinced it's the timid young countess.

The Old Woman Timeline and Summary

- The old woman is in the custodians' quarters with the narrator and the man with the withered arm, staring into the fire.
- The old woman tells the narrator that at 28 he still has a lot to see.
- The old woman exclaims twice "this night of all nights!" at intervals in the conversation between the narrator and the man with the withered arm.
- The next morning, the narrator finds the old woman taking care of him.
- When the narrator announces that the red room is indeed haunted, the old woman wants to know if the countess haunts it.

The Old Earl Character Analysis

The earl is one of the candidates for ghost of the red room, according to the custodians. A former master of Lorraine Castle, he apparently killed his wife in the red room when some joke of his went horribly wrong.

The Timid Young Countess Character Analysis

The countess is the other most likely candidate for the ghost haunting the red room, and the younger wife of the old earl. She apparently died in the red room as the result of some misguided joke her husband tried to play on her. According to legend, that's what started the whole haunting mess. Is she the woman the man with the shade refers to at the end of the story?

The Poor Young Duke Character Analysis

The poor young duke, whom the narrator mentions, was apparently the last person who tried to spend the night in the red room. Like the narrator who admires him, his aim was to prove that room wasn't haunted. He didn't end well: he died by falling down the spiral staircase at the entrance of the red room. The custodians blame his death on the haunted room, but the narrator thinks it was apoplexy.

Character Roles

Protagonist
The Narrator/Reason
No surprises here. The narrator is the guy with the heroic quest He wants to prove that the red room isn't haunted by spending the night in the room. He and his trusty candles represent the forces of light pitched against the forces of darkness. We have numerous such forces: the ghost that supposedly haunts the red room, the fear that actually haunts it, and the literal darkness. He's also the central character, the only character we know much about, and the character around whom the plot centers.

Actually, you could make the case that the protagonist is not just the narrator, but also the narrator's reason. Fear, which is definitely the antagonist, is something within the narrator. The narrator's fear struggles against his reason. It's the narrator's reason that gets "crushed" (45) by the darkness. Once this happens, he goes bananas and knocks himself unconscious.

That might be making things a little abstract, and it might not work so well in other respects: the narrator's literal fight against the darkness with candles is certainly his own attempt to control his fear, but it's not obvious how you could say his reason is fighting against the darkness. On the other hand, the narrator clearly identifies with his reason over his irrational fear. By making the narrator's reason the protagonist (or one of the protagonists), you can frame the story as an epic conflict between Reason and Fear that bears on all mankind.

Antagonist
Fear

The narrator's real battle in the story isn't with another character, but with whatever it is that haunts the room. It's fear that haunts the room, and fear that the narrator has to fight within himself. He also combats it physically, since the darkness of the room is both the cause and the symbol of his fear (see "Symbols, Imagery, Allegory" for more). It's against fear that the narrator and his reason lose their battle. (Recall that he tries to ward off the darkness with his candles.) It is ultimately Fear, which almost kills him (well, fear plus whatever it is he runs into). Fear is then presented at the story's end as the universal enemy of human reason and of human beings themselves.

Foil

The Narrator and the Custodians

We have a young, brash fellow who doesn't take superstition seriously on the one hand, and sketchy-looking older people, who are terrified of superstition, on the other. It's a pretty obvious contrast, but it's still an important one. This contrast helps frame the story's central conflict between fear and human reason. In the end, it turns out that the older people were right to be afraid, and that the narrator was wrong to be overly confident in his ability to master his fear. (Although, the custodians were wrong about what haunts the red room.)

Character Clues

Thoughts and Opinions

We're completely in the narrator's mind. That's good, because we know almost nothing about his "outer" characteristics or his circumstances – what he's wearing, where he's from, what he looks like, even what his name is – and he spends most of the story by himself. From his thoughts, however, we know that he's perhaps a little overconfident, that he gives a great value to being rational, that he looks down on superstition, that he has something against things which seem outdated, and that he is, in spite of himself, pretty easily freaked. That's just about all we need, isn't it?

Physical Appearances

We don't know what the narrator looks like. Since he is the singular focus of the story, the "Physical Appearances" category doesn't apply to him. On the other hand, for the three minor characters – the old custodians – we get the most information about their looks. For example, we get detailed descriptions of their pale eyes, decaying yellow teeth, and withered body parts. The two old men are even referred to by their physical deformities ("the man with the withered arm" and "the man with the shade"). For the narrator, the "spectral looks" (28) of the three custodians reflects their belonging to another age, where superstition reigned supreme. That they seem to belong to another age contrasts the custodians with the narrator, who looks youthful. Beyond that, though, the old custodians' looks don't tell us much about their characters. Their other role is to add the atmosphere and ambience to the story.

Actions

The narrator's decision to stay in the red room reveals some of his most important characteristics: he's daring (or arrogant), aims to be rational, and disregards superstition, committed to taking a stand against it. Once he's forced to walk the walk, however, his actions

also reveal his weak nerves and nervous disposition. Even before he reaches the red room, it's telling that he instinctively reaches for his revolver when he sees the Ganymede statue in the dark. We can tell that he's getting jumpy. His nervous rhyming once he's in the room, and his placement of a candle in the alcove, (because the shadows are getting to him), further testify to his fear. Then, there are those three screams when he really loses it. Admittedly, the narrator's actions aren't really so distinct from his thoughts, since he's the narrator and usually tells us what he's thinking or feeling about something as he does it.

Literary Devices

Symbols, Imagery, Allegory

Light and Darkness, Reason and Fear

It's a Gothic standard to contrast "the light" and "the darkness" or "the shadow." The whole work is supposed to seem "dark," foreboding, threatening, and mysterious. This usually means that the darkness is what prevails, and the light is either weak and isolated or completely absorbed. "Red Room" is no exception; it's chock full of this stuff. You want "overwhelming darkness"? It doesn't get much better than this:

And looking around that large sombre room, with its shadowy window bays, its recesses and alcoves, one could well understand the legends that had sprouted in its black corners, its germinating darkness. My candle was a little tongue of light in its vastness, that failed to pierce the opposite end of the room, and left an ocean of mystery and suggestion beyond its island of light. (31)

The whole house, and particularly the red room, is dark. This darkness threatens the narrator, because he doesn't know what might be lurking in it. It suggests dangers to him that aren't really there. In the dark, the narrator first thinks the statue of Ganymede and the Eagle in the hallway is "someone crouching to waylay" him (29). And then of course there are the shadows, which have "that undefinable quality of a presence, that odd suggestion of a lurking, living thing" (33). The darkness that inspires fear, and the "Fear" itself are intimately connected.

The narrator's own internal struggle against his fear is mirrored in his physical struggle with the darkness of the room. As a result, you can see *Fear/Darkness* and *Reason/Light* as closely connected pairs. By filling the red room with candlelight and illuminating its dark recesses (particularly the alcove), the narrator gives himself a sense of security and keeps his fear at bay. Reason, like light, is something that reveals. Reason is supposed to eliminate darkness or obscurity, to show that what's really there is not scary. When the candles begin to go out, the narrator engages in a literal fight against darkness as he tries to keep the room lit. As he becomes overwhelmed by darkness, the narrator grows increasingly frightened and loses his self-control. When the light is completely gone, so too are "the last vestiges of reason:"

…darkness closed upon me like the shutting of an eye, wrapped about me in a stifling embrace, sealed my vision, and crushed the last vestiges of reason from my brain. (45)

Fittingly, the story ends in the daytime, when the darkness is gone and the narrator can come back to his senses. In the light of day, he can realize what he was really fighting in the room.

Personifications of Darkness and Fear

Both fear and darkness are frequently described as active, threatening forces in the story. For darkness, you can take your pick from any number of descriptions:

- *The shadow in the alcove at the end in particular, had that undefinable quality of a presence, that odd suggestion of a lurking, living thing...*(33)
- *...the black shadow sprang back to its place there.*(37)
- *While I stood gaping, the candle at the foot of the bed went out, and the shadows seemed to take another step towards me.* (39)
- *...darkness closed upon me like the shutting of an eye, wrapped about me in a stifling embrace...*(45)

As for fear, it gets the dramatic quotes at the end of the story:

- *"Fear that will not have light nor sound, that will not bear with reason, that deafens and darkens and overwhelms. It followed me through the corridor, it fought against me in the room----"* (57)
- *It lurks there always. You can feel it even in the daytime, even of a bright summer's day, in the hangings, in the curtains, keeping behind you however you face about. In the dusk it creeps along the corridor and follows you, so that you dare not turn.* (60)

What's the deal with all of this personification of two abstract, nonliving things? Well, first, it certainly sounds cool. More importantly, though, it helps Wells give metaphorical meat to one of the story's big ideas. Fear is uncontrollable, and is almost like an active evil force or spirit in the way it can strike at human beings and render them helpless. What better way to do that than describing it as alive? And since darkness and fear are so closely connected in the story, why not do it for both?

In addition, giving life to the darkness also lets us more directly into the narrator's nervous state of mind: his fear makes him see threatening figures in the darkness and leads him to feel that there is some dark power actively attacking him.

The Statue of Ganymede and the Eagle

In case you're wondering, Ganymede was a character in Greek mythology, a boy who was more beautiful than any other mortal. That's why one day he was snatched up by Zeus (the king of the gods). Zeus turned himself into an eagle and plucked unsuspecting Ganymede off the ground to fly him back to Mount Olympus (home of the gods). Zeus made Ganymede the gods' cupbearer, and granted him immortality.

Anyway, you might figure that since Wells mentions this specific myth in the story with the statue it must mean something. We would too, but we can't come up with anything that's not overly vague or slightly fishy. There is something threatening or ominous about the myth, in that Ganymede is taken without any warning by a force outside of his control (a big eagle would be

scary enough in itself). Maybe you could see Ganymede's powerlessness before a higher, threatening power as mirroring the narrator's powerlessness before fear and the unknown? Maybe H.G. Wells just thought a big eagle would cast a particularly creepy statue in the dark? Do you have any ideas about the significance of this statue?

Setting

The Haunted Red Room in Lorraine Castle

The story takes place at night in creepy Lorraine Castle, which has presumably been around for quite a while. These days it's abandoned, and has been for eighteen months, although we don't know why. Apparently, the former owner, mentioned only as "her ladyship," died. Now only the three eerie old custodians take care of the place.

Where is Lorraine Castle, and when is the story set? Lorraine also happens to be a region in France where there are several castles in close proximity, but we have absolutely no reason to think that our English speaking characters are set in France. To make a long story short, we don't know where Lorraine Castle is located. Though apparently, according to the old woman, the night when the story takes place ("This night of all nights!" [16, 23]) has some special significance. Maybe the young countess died on the same night years ago?

The castle's interior is dark, dusty, and filled with spooky stuff. The spookiest place of all is the red room, the supposedly haunted room where the narrator spends the night. It has a tragic history, because various people have died there (we don't get many details). In particular, something horrible seems to have happened to a timid young countess because of a failed joke her husband played. The room is also enormous, done in red and black, with plenty of large bay windows and "recesses and alcoves" (31) where darkness lingers and suggestive shadows seem to come alive. At one end is a fireplace, and at the other end is an alcove. Because the alcove is farthest from the firelight, it is particularly dark, and is the favored spot for those "living, lurking" (33) shadows that make the narrator so nervous. Definitely creepy.

The room's creepiness is actually very important to the story, because of the effect it has on the narrator. Everything about it – its coloring, its imposing size, its history, its darkness – is perfect for inducing fear, and it does. It's that "Fear!" which haunts the room and overwhelms the narrator. Not only is the room the arena of the narrator's "struggle against darkness" and Fear, it is itself intimately bound up with them.

Narrator Point of View

First Person

A nameless narrator tells us of his own experiences in the red room firsthand. The first person narrative is actually indispensable for the story, since Wells's main interest is exploring the psychology of the narrator. Telling the story first-personally allows him to reveal, bit by bit, the

narrator's transition from mild jumpiness to mindless terror. We also get to see the constant conflict between what the narrator tells himself, and what he's actually feeling. The first person perspective also puts the reader herself in more direct contact with the narrator's fear, making it easier to catch some of his state of mind.

Additionally, the first-person narration prevents the reader from ever knowing with certainty what's really happening. There's no omniscient presence to say, as the candles go out, that it's really just the wind. Or, for that matter, there's no one to confirm the narrator's diagnosis that the room is haunted by Fear. We never know whether or not there is a ghost. We have to take the narrator's word for it.

Genre

Gothic/Horror, Psychological Thriller

"The Red Room" has all the basics of a work of horror: a plot revolving around the supernatural, an atmosphere of looming threat, a terror-filled narrator (whose case of the creeps is supposed to carry over to the reader), sharp contrasts between feeble light and ever-present darkness (think the candle imagery: "its germinating darkness. My candle was a little tongue of light in its vastness…" [31]).

But that's not all. The story seems almost deliberately designed to include some attributes of 19th century Gothic fiction. You might recognize some of these characteristics; Gothic works still abide in pop culture today. Here we have: an old, abandoned mansion said to be haunted; the tragic history which is only barely hinted at; those ominous, old custodians with fire-lit faces who say things like "This night of all nights!" (16, 23); long moonlit hallways with weird statues that cast suggestive shadows; candles that blow out at exactly the wrong moment; need we continue?

Where Wells goes beyond the genre is in the psychological aspect of his work. The struggle of the hero and the "powers of darkness" are turned inward; the story becomes a conflict between the narrator's reason, and a terror that threatens to overwhelm his intellect. You might even say Wells turns the Gothic genre on its head. Although Gothic stories deal often enough with the psychology of fear, the focus is usually on what causes the fear. More often than not, this turns out to be a supernatural element, which may or may not be real. If it is real, then we can heave a sigh of relief: there's no reason to have been afraid after all. Wells's story implies that fear itself is what matters. If there is only fear, then there can be no relief; fear itself is an active, evil power that threatens to destroy human beings. It's something we can't control but must fight. From the experience of the narrator in the red room, we see that this fight is easily lost. Using a whole slew of the genre's own classic images, Wells suggests that Gothic fiction may have missed the point and, overlooked the real "power of darkness," and the scariest thing of all.

Tone

Precisely analytical and slightly disdainful, with a dose of foreboding and a pinch of hysteria

As "The Red Room" is told in the first person, the tone reflects the attitude of the main character. The narrator's determination to be "rational" comes across in the ordered, detailed, analytical, and somewhat removed descriptions he gives. This applies not only to the house and the things he sees. But it also applies to the narrator's own mental states, and the motivations behind his actions. Doesn't this just sound like a scientist: "I resolved to make a systematic examination of the place at once, and dispel the fanciful suggestions of its obscurity before they obtained a hold upon me" (32). Because of the narrator's commitment to being rational and clear-headed, he looks down upon anything that seems superstitious or fantastic. This disdain comes across in his dismissal of the "fanciful suggestion" of the room. Or the old people, who he says are prey to "fashions born in dead brains" (28).

In spite of his claims to being rational, a nervousness and sense of foreboding does creep into the narrator's tone as the story progresses. We see this first in the unease and mysterious suggestiveness of some of his descriptions, as when he says the shadows in the red room make "that odd suggestion of a lurking, living thing" (33). As he grows more frightened, we see shorter sentences and more frantic, exaggerated language: "I leaped panting and disheveled from candle to candle, in a vain struggle against that remorseless advance" (43). Still, by the time the narrator gets knocked unconscious, we're a long way from over-the-top hysteria, and the tone maintains a certain distance from the utter panic the narrator is feeling at that moment.

Writing Style

Structured, Ornate, Prone to Occasional Flights of Fancy

Wells's writing is certainly well ordered. His sentences and paragraphs are always neatly divided and structured in a point-by-point way fashion that complements the narrator's analytical tone. But that doesn't mean the writing is simple or terse. Wells is a late 19th century British writer, and not afraid of indulging in some pretty fanciful multi-part sentences. Check out this one with seven clauses (follow the commas – they keep it organized):

I entered, closed the door behind me at once, turned the key I found in the lock within, and stood with the candle held aloft, surveying the scene of my vigil, the great red room of Lorraine Castle, in which the young duke had died. (31)

This kind of sentence can lend an air of pretension to the writing. So too does Wells's word choice. He often tends towards old-fashioned words, (i.e., "foregathered" – [28]), and frequent use of overdone modifiers, as in "absolute silence" (28) or "marvelous distinctness" (29). (We admit, we find it kind of charming). And then, every so often, Wells will just hit you with something totally over the top: "My candle was a little tongue of light in its vastness, that failed to pierce the opposite end of the room, and left an ocean of mystery and suggestion beyond its

island of light" (31). "Ocean of mystery" and "island of light"? Kind of beautiful, but for some people that sort of imagery could sound just a little too epic. And how about that "germinating darkness" (31)?

What's Up With the Title?

The title is pretty straightforward: the haunted locale around which the story revolves is "The Red Room." That title grabs you, doesn't it? And not just because it's short and alliterative (repeating the same sound). It's all about the *red*. You see a lot of white rooms, or blue rooms, or yellow rooms, probably because they're comforting colors that easily fade into the background and just become "ambience." (How about that drab hospital green?) You *don't* see a lot of red rooms. Red is loud, attention getting, the kind of thing that makes a serious statement. Even if there is a red room in a house, chances are that room is a living room or kitchen, and not a bedroom. Would you want to sleep in a red room? And just think of all the eerie associations. You hear "red room" and you might think of bloodstained walls, or fire. Or something even worse: red wallpaper loud enough to drive a person crazy.

What's Up With the Ending?

The ending of "The Red Room" is classic. What turns out to haunt the room? Drum roll...fear itself. And that killer last quote: "There is Fear in that room of hers – black Fear, and there will be – so long as this house of sin endures" (60). Can't you just see the 40's horror movie, with Boris Karloff delivering that line right as the credits come on to spooky music?

There's quite a suspenseful buildup to the ending until the narrator announces what it is that really haunts the red room. We still never know what *actually* happened to the narrator up there. Was it all in his mind, or was there *actually* a ghost? When he tells the others that the room is "haunted," it sounds as if he's going to concede, and admit – against what he said at the beginning – that there really is a ghost. But he doesn't. The room is haunted by *fear*. No ghosts in this story.

Now you might think: "It's just fear? I wanted a ghost!" Not so fast. If we take the ending seriously, what's in the room isn't "just" fear, it's FEAR! Fear is far more terrifying than anything we could imagine. It's dangerous. Fear killed the young duke, (who apparently fell down the stairs), and almost killed the narrator by making them lose their senses, and they couldn't do anything to control it. That might be worse than your garden-variety ghost could manage. And what's more, in spite of his initial boasting, didn't the narrator lose the battle with fear? He couldn't beat it. It's just his luck that he didn't fall down the stairs or otherwise mortally injure himself, like the duke did.

What about the dire pronouncement the man with the shades makes at the end? He proclaims that the red room will remain haunted by Fear until the house is gone. We think this suggests something else about fear. Fear isn't just in one's head; we should actually take that language of it *haunting* a place seriously. The eerie atmosphere and the dreadful history of the red room combine to make it a place that will scare whoever visits it, even if they "know" it's not really haunted. What happened to the narrator will happen to anyone else who tries. Each additional

person's defeat by fear in the red room will only increase its frightful reputation.

If you're also wondering about why the man with the shade speaks of the room being "that room of hers," you'll have to keep guessing. He must be referring to the young countess, but by the story's end we still don't know what happened to her.

One last thing: it's interesting to note that both the narrator and the man with the shades personify fear (in addition to putting it in capital letters). Fear "followed" the narrator, and "fought" against him in the room, while the man with the shades speaks of it "lurking" and "creeping." That adds extra effect to the idea we've just developed. Rather than being "merely psychological," it might be more accurate to think of fear as an actively hostile force, which terrorizes individual people. Not that different from a ghost after all.

When all's said and done, you might still feel let down about there being no ghost. In which case, here's something else to think about. We get the conclusion that there is no ghost from the narrator, but it's not clear how he knows that. Sure he and the guy with the shades, and almost certainly Wells himself (who's trying to make a point), think there's no real ghost. But what was blowing out all of those candles? What took care of the fire just when the narrator needed it? We didn't have any mention of wind, besides one measly draft that makes one of the candles flicker (i.e., not nearly powerful enough to blow out multiple candles). And did the narrator really get so battered just from crashing into things? "The Red Room" answers none of these questions.

Did You Know?

Trivia

- H.G. Wells's first published book was a biology textbook (in 1893). (Source)
- Wells also wrote two concise works on the history of the world: *An Outline of World History* (1920) and *A Short History of the World* (1922). (Source)
- Wells was, for a time, a passionate socialist (though not a Marxist), an outspoken believer in "utopia," and a member of Britain's famous socialist club, the Fabian Society. He wrote many nonfiction works expressing these views. (Source)
- Wells actually fought for control over the Fabian Society against another famous author, playwright George Bernard Shaw. (Source)
- A portion of H.G. Wells's famous book, *War of the Worlds*, once created a national panic in the United States. On October 30, 1938, Orson Welles, a popular radiobroadcaster read a script over the air based on the episode from the book in which the Martians first land and begin their invasion of earth. Millions of Americans believed a real Martian invasion was underway. (Source)
- Wells is often credited with imagining various scientific advances before they happened. Most famously, he "predicted" the atomic bomb in a 1914 work of fiction called *The World Set Free*. (Source)
- Embittered during World War II, which he claimed to have warned the world about, Wells

once threatened that his epitaph would read: "I told you so. You *damned* fools." (Source)

Steaminess Rating

G
Unlike many recent horror movies and novels, there is not any sex at all in this story.

Best of the Web

Websites
"The Red Room"
http://books.google.com/books?id=Q_wNAAAAYAAJ&pg=PA31&dq=The+Red+Room+Wells
A good online edition of the story.

H.G. Wells on BBC
http://www.bbc.co.uk/southerncounties/content/articles/2007/08/22/h_is_for_hgwells_feature.shtml
A great Wells page about his origins.

Wells on Project Gutenberg
http://www.gutenberg.org/browse/authors/w#a30
All of Wells's works available for download on Project Gutenberg.

Audio
The Red Room Audiobook
http://literalsystems.org/litsys/audio/Audio-Book/TheRedRoom.mp3
Hear the story read aloud, and nicely, by Simon Teolis.

H.G. Wells meets Orson Welles
http://www.youtube.com/watch?v=nUdghSMTXsU
A great old radio clip with a meeting of the two great Wells. Hear H.G. Wells' voice!

Images
H.G. Wells
http://www.freepedia.co.uk/The%20Web%20Site%20Backup/Writers/JwellsH.jpg
A classic photo of the author.

H.G. Wells in 1932
http://www.worldandi.com/newhome/public/2004/january/graphics/Bk2pub3.jpg

Another great Wells shot.

32429539R00024

Printed in Great Britain
by Amazon